Before you start ...

1 Read all the instructions for the activity. Gather together the equipment you need using the list at the top of the page. When choosing plants, check what growing conditions they like best.

2 Cover your worktable with newspaper. Put on an apron and wear gardening gloves when handling soil.

3 Be patient. Plants take time to grow. Water them regularly, pick off dead flower heads, and feed them with plant food.

4 Be careful with scissors. Only use them if an adult is there to help you.

5 When you have finished, put away your garden tools, clean up, and wash your hands.

DK

A DK PUBLISHING BOOK

Written and edited by Dawn Sirett and Lara Tankel
Art Editors Mandy Earey and Mary Sandberg
Additional design Veneta Altham
Deputy Managing Art Editor C. David Gillingwater
US Editor Camela Decaire
Production Fiona Baxter
Dib, Dab, and Dob made by Wilfrid Wood
Photography by Alex Wilson and Norman Hollands
Illustrations by Peter Kavanagh

First American Edition, 1997
2 4 6 8 10 9 7 5 3 1

Published in the United States by DK Publishing, Inc.
95 Madison Avenue, New York, New York 10016

Copyright © 1997 Dorling Kindersley Limited, London
Visit us on the World Wide Web at http://www.dk.com

Published in Great Britain by Dorling Kindersley Ltd.

A CIP catalog record for this book is
available from the Library of Congress.

ISBN 0-7894-1523-2

Color reproduction by Colourscan, Singapore
Printed and bound in Hong Kong by Imago

PLAY AND LEARN

Growing Things

With Dib, Dab, and Dob

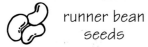 runner bean seeds

 bowl of water

 paper towel

jar

 watering can

Grow a runner bean

Water the beans whenever the paper feels dry.

Leave a few runner bean seeds in a bowl of water overnight.

The next day, push a paper towel inside a jar.

Put your beans in the jar against the paper towel. Water them and put the jar in a sunny place.

 gardening gloves trowel flowerpot potting soil 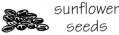 sunflower seeds

See a sunflower grow

Fill a pot with soil. Push
a sunflower seed into
the soil and water the
soil lightly.

Put the
pot in a sunny
place. Water
when dry.

Soon a shoot will appear.
When it grows tall, push
a stake into the soil and
tie the shoot to the stake.

watering can

bamboo stake and ties

felt-tip pen

Every week, mark the height of the sunflower on the stake.

How high does your sunflower grow?

 gardening gloves trowel  window box gravel potting soil

Plant a window box

I need more soil, Dab.

Put a thin layer of gravel in a window box.

Then fill the box with soil.

A blooming garden

Water your plants every day in summer.

cotton saucer cookie cutter  seeds for sprouting  watering can

Grow and eat sprouting seeds

Put some cotton on a saucer. Place a cookie cutter on top and sprinkle the seeds inside it.

Make sure everything is really wet, Dib.

Soak the cotton and seeds. Put the saucer on a windowsill and water the seeds every day.

 florist's foam

 plastic bowl

 basket

scissors

 fresh flowers

Arrange a flower basket

Wet some foam and put it in a plastic bowl. Place the bowl in a basket.

Ask an adult to trim the stems of some flowers.

The tallest flowers look best in the middle.

Push the flowers into the foam.

foliage

Then fill the gaps
with some foliage.

 gardening gloves trowel  shallow plant container gravel potting soil

Grow a beach garden

Put a thin layer of gravel in a plant container.

I think that's enough soil.

Cover the gravel with lots of soil.

Choose some plants for your beach garden and dig holes for them.

small plants*
and decoration

sand
and spoon

watering
can

Put the
plants in
the holes.
Press
around
them.

Spoon on
some sand and
add a few
shells.

*Choose plants such
is succulents or grasses.

Rocky gardens

Put your garden in a
sunny place and water
it to settle the plants.
From then on, water
it only if
the soil
is dry.